How to Write a Poem:

A Beginner's Guide

Sean O'Neill

Sean O'Neill

2

For Liz

Sean O'Neill

TABLE OF CONTENTS

Introduction

You might want to write a poem for a special occasion, like someone's birthday, or to record a particular event, or even just because you feel an emotion strongly. For whatever the reason, many of us feel the need - and sometimes it is a need – to occasionally write some poetry. The crucial question is: How do you write a poem? This question has a long pedigree and it has been answered throughout history by a number of authors. Aristotle's "Treatise on Poetry," Horace's "Art of Poetry", and Sir Philip Sidney's "The Defense of Poesie," are all works that seek to answer this question.

This is a practical book. By the time you finish reading it, you will have all the tools you need to write convincing, compelling, and beautiful poetry. Whether someone has asked you to come up with a poem for a special occasion, or you have suddenly been struck by an intense emotion and are looking for a way to articulate it, or you want to express love to your sweetheart on Valentine's day, this book provides all the necessary techniques to enable your poem to be a success.

Here are some of the other questions this book answers: Can anyone write a poem or is it an ability that the chosen few are born with? Where do you start? How do you come up with an idea for a poem? Should you use a formal style like a sonnet, which has a strict set of rules that should be adhered to, or opt for free verse, where, it seems as if anything goes? And once you've written a poem, how can you tell if it's any good?

With copious examples from some of the greats of poetry this book is packed full of useful advice to get you started on the road to writing poetry.

(NB. Any unattributed poems in this book are the work of the author.)

Chapter 1 - What is a Poem?

Good question. And it's not one to which there is a definitive answer. Nevertheless, broadly speaking a poem, like a song, is almost always immediately recognized on paper. This is because it is probably written in stanzas or paragraphs, it may rhyme – or it may not. It will often use metaphors and similes – comparing things that are not usually compared with each other. Sometimes a poem will have a set meter – a pattern of stresses and beats that the words follow. However, it is not too difficult to come up with poems that go against this description, but can still be called poems.

Traditionally, poetry was meant to be spoken aloud. This tradition goes back probably for almost as long as humans have been able to speak. In the Middle Ages, bards and troubadours used to tour the countryside and sing or recite ballads and poems to rich people for money. Nowadays, poets still give readings of their own poetry to groups here and there throughout the country. So it seems there has always been a history of poetry being spoken aloud.

Poetry is, therefore, fundamentally about communication. That's not to say that you can't sit down privately and write poems just for your own amusement or in order to express some deeply felt emotion (but always, perhaps, with the faint hope that someone somewhere will stumble upon your work and hail it as a masterpiece!).

The nature of poetry is that it should be shared with

others and so, to that extent, it is always useful to have in mind an imaginary audience: someone, or a group of people, to whom we are writing or that we hope will read our poem once we have finished writing it. Even if we never end up showing our poem to someone else, it's still a good discipline to write the best we can for that ethereal but sympathetic entity: the imaginary audience. It focuses what we are writing, eradicates the compulsion to babble or gush with excess emotion and, more often than not, makes the finished product more pleasing and accomplished than it would otherwise have been.

Ok, enough about what a poem is. How do I write one?

Choosing a Subject

How do you pick a subject for your poem? Some subjects seem to pick us. Sometimes we are so struck by the sadness or the delightfulness of a scene or an event that we want to write about it. Failing that, however, there are several main areas we can explore to come up with a theme.

Place: Think of somewhere you have been that has had an effect on you. It might be an abandoned warehouse, or a room in the home in which you grew up, or a bridge over a river, or a city just before dawn. W.B. Yeats's poem "The Lake Isle of Innisfree" is an example of how a place can take on a character of its own through your poetry. It begins:

I will arise and go now, and go to Innisfree,
And a small cabin build there, of clay and wattles made;
Nine bean-rows will I have there, a hive for the honey-bee,
And live alone in the bee-loud glade.

A past experience: Any kind of experience can be used. For example sitting an exam, going for a walk, losing your phone, running for a train, being told that someone you know has died. John Milton's long poem "Lycidas" was written on the occasion of the poet, Edward King's, death. It begins:

Yet once more, O ye laurels, and once more
Ye myrtles brown, with ivy never sere,
I come to pluck your berries harsh and crude,
And with forc'd fingers rude
Shatter your leaves before the mellowing year.
Bitter constraint and sad occasion dear
Compels me to disturb your season due;
For Lycidas is dead, dead ere his prime,
Young Lycidas, and hath not left his peer.

A particular person: This could be someone related to you, or a complete stranger you pass in the street. It might be someone famous, or a historical figure, or a traffic cop, a friend or an enemy. A lot of poems that are directed at a specific person, for example love poems, say a lot about the person writing them. John Donne's love poem "Twickenham Gardens" has that quality, where the poet expresses, more than anything else, self-reproach. It begins:

BLASTED with sighs, and surrounded with tears,
Hither I come to seek the spring,
And at mine eyes, and at mine ears,
Receive such balms as else cure every thing.
But O! self-traitor, I do bring
The spider Love, which transubstantiates all,
And can convert manna to gall ;
And that this place may thoroughly be thought
True paradise, I have the serpent brought.

An object: This might be anything as varied as a cup of coffee or a child's toy. It could be a car, the sun, a desk, a melon or a house porch. The poem, "The Day My Car Died," whose subject is what it sounds like, begins:

A point of gunmetal gray
tarnished by the workhorse years
a flange, a nipple, a block
enclose the miracle of movement
under the black hood.

Ratchet, piston, valve, plug
plot out their kinetic wonder
beating out microscopic failure
in a matter of time
if only time were good.

An emotion: often the reason someone might want to write a poem in the first place is because of an emotion, whether it be hate or love, embarrassment or contentment, excitement or sadness. Allen Ginsberg's classic poem,

"Howl" is a long rant full of anger, but is nevertheless very effective poetically. Here's a short section from the beginning:

I saw the best minds of my generation destroyed by madness, starving hysterical naked,
dragging themselves through the negro streets at dawn looking for an angry fix,
angelheaded hipsters burning for the ancient heavenly connection to the starry dynamo in the machinery of night,
who poverty and tatters and hollow-eyed and high sat up smoking in the supernatural darkness of cold-water flats floating across the tops of cities contemplating jazz...

An event: You could write about a wedding of someone you know, a funeral you attended, a football game in which your team won or an election that had a surprise outcome. Here's a snippet from a sonnet that is simply called "The Wedding."

The man stood, stolidly to attention
up front. There were, in the church's narthex,
presentiments of crying or car wrecks
to account for the bride's absence. Tension
stalked down the aisles like a collection plate.
Then murmurs, crushed silk, sighs, and they began.
The organ played the march, she almost ran,
and white married gray at long last, though late.

A landscape or seascape scene: This topic gives you a lot of scope to describe different types of trees, grass swaying in the wind, waves lapping on the shore, the horizon melting into the land, an angry sky, misty mountains and hills. The free-verse poem "Cairngarroch Beach," describes the shoreline near a fishing village on the west coast of Scotland.

> The wheedling of the great sea
> bent down upon the nose of the shore,
> clogged with rotting kelp and the clutter
>
> of a thousand frantic visitors,
> and spent the balance of days
> breaking the rocks all to sand.
>
> When I took the swoop of the road
> down to the beach, seagulls
> were fighting over garbage
>
> or a spill of shellfish on the pier,
> and where I looked out under my hand
> the breakers were rolling in to the birthplace.

A time of year: Some of the most famous poems have been about endless summers, or harsh and brutal winters. But you could also write about someone's birthday – and give the poem to them as a birthday gift, or about Christmas, Hanukkah or New Year's Day. Thomas Hardy's "The Darkling Thrush" commemorated the turn of the century over a hundred years ago. Here is stanza two, by way of example:

The land's sharp features seemed to be
The Century's corpse outleant,
His crypt the cloudy canopy,
The wind his death-lament.
The ancient pulse of germ and birth
Was shrunken hard and dry,
And every spirit upon earth
Seemed fervourless as I.

A time of day: This subject can include getting up in the morning full of life and energy, going to bed at night exhausted (or vice versa if you're on night shift!); the regularity of the working day or the peace of leisure time; watching a glorious sunrise or sunset. Walt Whitman's "I Hear America Singing" celebrates work at various times of day. Here are a few lines from the poem:

I hear America singing, the varied carols I hear,
Those of mechanics, each one singing his as it should be blithe and strong,
The carpenter singing his as he measures his plank or beam,
The mason singing his as he makes ready for work, or leaves off work,
The boatman singing what belongs to him in his boat, the deckhand singing on the steamboat deck,
The shoemaker singing as he sits on his bench, the hatter singing as he stands...

Weather: Deafening thunderstorms, sinister fog, a day under the scorching sun, a day of miserable drizzle, an overcast or cloudy day, heavy snow, pelting hail, lashing rain and wind: any one of these could play a part in your poem. T.S. Eliot has a much quoted image of fog as a dog from "The Lovesong of J. Alfred Prufrock":

The yellow fog that rubs its back upon the window-panes,
The yellow smoke that rubs its muzzle on the window-panes
Licked its tongue into the corners of the evening,
Lingered upon the pools that stand in drains,
Let fall upon its back the soot that falls from chimneys,
Slipped by the terrace, made a sudden leap,
And seeing that it was a soft October night,
Curled once about the house, and fell asleep.

An animal: This can be a domestic animal like a dog or cat, or something exotic like a gorilla or a snake. I often find it useful to do some background research on a particular animal to give me some material to work with. "Baby Tortoise," by D.H. Lawrence is a good example of an animal poem. It begins:

You know what it is to be born alone,
Baby tortoise!

The first day to heave your feet little by little from
the shell,
Not yet awake,
And remain lapsed on earth,
Not quite alive.

A tiny, fragile, half-animate bean.

An activity: This can range from harvest time in the fields to filling out a tax form; from fixing a car to shaking someone by the hand; and from painting a wall to roller-skating down a hill. Here's the first part of Wilfred Owen's painfully poignant poem "Dulce et Decorum Est" about walking back to the barracks after a day fighting during the First World War:

Bent double, like old beggars under sacks,
Knock-kneed, coughing like hags, we cursed through sludge,
Till on the haunting flares we turned our backs,
And towards our distant rest began to trudge.
Men marched asleep. Many had lost their boots,
But limped on, blood-shod. All went lame; all blind;
Drunk with fatigue; deaf even to the hoots
Of gas-shells dropping softly behind.

A piece of music or a work of art: The poet William Carlos Williams wrote a poem based on Breughel's painting, "Landscape with the Fall of Icarus" and John Keats wrote his "Ode on a Grecian Urn." Robert Pinsky wrote "Street Music" and John Dryden his "The Power of Music." Music and art, therefore, are quite legitimate subject matter for a poem. Here's part of a poem on the famous painting by Picasso depicting the massacre that took place in the Basque village of Guernica:

When Pablo has word about the raid,
his outrage blooms into twisted
bodies, tortured faces and limbs.

He takes one day to calmly sketch
and by evening all the elements
coalesce into finality.

His arm, like a conduit of rage,
describes the overarching doom
of the seventeen hundred dead.

Some ran. Others died where they
stood, in fractured shards of bone
and grayscale evisceration.

An anecdote or narrative: Your memory holds an immense font of anecdotes or happenings from the past. In addition to that, we have stories that have been reported to us by other people. Any one of these could be the subject of a poem. In the following excerpt Alfred, Lord Tennyson describes "The Charge of the Light Brigade" which was a British light cavalry charge led by Lord Cardigan against Russian forces during the Battle of Balaclava on 25 October 1854 in the Crimean War.

Half a league, half a league,
Half a league onward,
All in the valley of Death
Rode the six hundred.
"Forward, the Light Brigade!
"Charge for the guns!" he said:
Into the valley of Death
Rode the six hundred.

"Forward, the Light Brigade!"
Was there a man dismay'd?
Not tho' the soldier knew
Someone had blunder'd:
Theirs not to make reply,
Theirs not to reason why,
Theirs but to do and die:
Into the valley of Death
Rode the six hundred.

Cannon to right of them,
Cannon to left of them,
Cannon in front of them
Volley'd and thunder'd;
Storm'd at with shot and shell,
Boldly they rode and well,
Into the jaws of Death,
Into the mouth of Hell
Rode the six hundred.

No doubt there are other categories and some subjects that span more than one category. However, it is important to have something to latch your words onto with a poem. Otherwise the poem can easily become vague and rambling and end up saying nothing much at all.

Chapter 2 - Where Do You Start?

Imagery

One of the things that separates poetry from prose is that poetry tends to use figurative language, or what is called "imagery," more often. Imagery is a method of using words or phrases in such a way that an impression or sensation is created in the readers' minds that allows them to experience, second-hand as it were, what the poet is expressing. The impressions created in the mind of the reader come from the five senses, sight, hearing, taste, smell and touch. There are a number of different techniques for developing imagery, most of which are covered in Chapter 3. For now, let's describe two of the most frequently used techniques – **metaphor** and **simile** – and then show how to use them in the creation of a poem.

What is a Metaphor?

A metaphor is a figure of speech in which a word or phrase is applied to an object or action to which it is not literally applicable. Examples are: "he sank into the pit of despair"; "she was on cloud nine with happiness"; "he was green with envy"; "her tongue was razor sharp". These examples are, of course, very familiar, if not hackneyed to death, and as a result not very effective. Good poetry contains apt, but fresh, metaphors, not clichés.

What is a Simile?

A simile is a figure of speech involving the comparison of one thing with another thing of a different kind, used to make a description more emphatic or vivid. It usually employs the words "like" or "as". Examples are: "the clouds hunched over like a weightlifter's back," "his frown was as tight as a clenched fist," "the day dragged on like a turtle on weed."

Getting started

Right, let's write a poem. First, choose a subject for your poem using the guidelines in Chapter 1. Now close your eyes and imagine yourself at a particular scene involving the subject of your poem. Use your senses. What do you see, hear, smell, touch, even taste? Can you bring these images to life for the reader by linking what you experience to some other thing (metaphor, or simile)? Write down what comes to mind. When writing a poem it is important to get the first few lines down, just to get started. Don't worry if they're not very good. You can always discard them later or go back and change them. The key is to make a start.

Poem Walkthrough

Here's an example of what I mean. I have decided to write a poem about standing out on the porch of a

21

country house watching the sunset. I close my eyes and imagine myself there.

What do I see? I see the sky gradually turning to red and the land darkening.

What do I hear? I hear the slight rustle of the trees and the birdsong gradually dying away.

What do I smell? I smell the aroma of new-mown grass and the faint scent of flowers.

What do I touch or feel? I feel the floor of the wooden porch beneath my feet and the breeze on my cheek.

What do I taste? I can taste the scotch and soda that I have in my glass (which is the reason why I'm in the mood to write a poem in the first place...)

Okay. Now we've collected a group of impressions, that we want to convey to the reader making use of figurative language. What can we do with them? Let's turn to simile for help. We see the sky reddening; what can we compare that to? Perhaps a blush on someone's cheek. So we can attempt the first few lines:

> *"The sky reddened like a blush*
> *And the land darkened*
> *As the sun dropped."*

Now what? Well, what do we hear? Birdsong dying away. What can we compare that to? Maybe dying soldiers? We also hear the rustle of trees. This time we'll use metaphor.

> *"The soldiers of birdsong died*
> *On the battlefield of the tree-murmuring sky."*

Except that "tree-murmuring" sounds a bit clumsy. What about "shattering". Okay, let's go with that.

*"The soldier of birdsong died
On the battlefield of the shattering sky."*

Also, let's go back and change the first line to:

"The sky reddened like a wound."

And let's change the second line to:

"And the land darkened with its blood."

Now it fits in much better with the idea of soldiers dying. The connotations of "wound" as opposed to "blush" are more violent and painful. And the addition of "blood" has similar connotations. The poem has taken an unexpected serious turn.

Next, what do I smell? Grass and flowers. So how do we work that in? Well, we don't want to belabor the metaphors and simile techniques so we could just plainly say:

*"The smell of grass and lilies
Lingers on the air"*

Now let's take the sense of touch. We can feel the wooden boards of the porch beneath our feet. The boards make a kind of old and mournful sound.

"While the deep-grained porch boards
Creak their old dirge of death
With the dying day,"

We can also feel the breeze on our cheek. Perhaps it's like someone whispering to us.

"And the breeze whispers of secrets
And the threat of the night."

And lastly we can taste the scotch, which reminds us of old friends.

"I swirl my glass of scotch
And think I taste the laughter,
Of old friends."

But we close out the poem with a reference back to the harshness of the start. We can change the last line to:

Of old friends. I stifle one bitter curse.

And there we have it! If we divide it into stanzas it could look like this:

The sky reddened like a wound.
And the land darkened with its blood
As the sun dropped.
The soldiers of birdsong died
On the battlefield of the shattering sky.

The smell of grass and lilies
Lingers on the air
While the deep-grained porch boards
Creak their old dirge of death
With the dying day,

And the breeze whispers of secrets
And the threat of the night.
I swirl my glass of scotch
And think I taste the laughter
Of old friends. I stifle one bitter curse.

It's certainly not Shakespeare, and it turned out to be about, well, death and perhaps betrayal. But it's a start. It is, of course, not necessary to use all the senses and it doesn't do to overuse metaphor and simile, but you can see the difference between the above poem and a piece of prose. Also, you can see how we went back and changed the first two lines so that they would fit in with the lines about soldiers dying. It's important to go back over a poem and tweak it here and there until you're happy with it. For example, the word "shattering" in the last line of the first stanza still doesn't quite work, and perhaps we could think of a better phrase than the slightly hackneyed "dying day" in the last line of the second stanza. It's fun to go back over a poem and try to perfect it. The inclusion of lilies, at the start of stanza two, fits in with the "death" theme (lilies are often used in funerals) and, because of the overall sadness of the poem and the bitter curse at the end, it makes us think that the "old friends" mentioned at the end may, in fact, have passed away or perhaps they have betrayed him and that is why they are laughing. You may also have noticed that the tense changes from past to present between the first and second stanzas. Using the present tense makes what you're saying more immediate and potentially more compelling.

Another piece of advice that is well worth considering is: keep the punch line for the end of your poem. In other words, the most powerful message of your poem should come at the end. In the case of the above poem, the writer's experience of the scene is summed up by the fact that it makes him think of past friends he knew who are no longer around.

On the other hand, the words you use to begin your poem are crucially important too. What you want to aim at is something that grabs the reader's attention, that gets to the point and doesn't waffle. In the above poem, the word "wound" in line one immediately alerts the reader to the fact that this is no ordinary peaceful sunset we're talking about. It draws the reader to read on. It is important to take into account the **connotations** of any metaphors or similes you use and to make sure that they are in keeping with the general tone of the poem.

This poem uses the pronoun "I" to describe the scene and to put forward certain sentiments. But the "I" here is really just a **persona** that I took on while writing the poem. It does not mean that this actually happened to me. So it is quite legitimate, while you are writing, to take on a persona or the voice of an imaginary person, or project yourself into an imagined – or even a real – scene. This technique has been used in countless poems and it is a very effective way of getting across some timeless truth or profound statement, without having to rely solely on your own experience of life.

By the way, as you can see I began each line with a capital letter. That used to be the rigid rule for poetry, but now it is permissible to only begin each sentence with a capital letter and leave the other line beginnings in lower case. Also, it must be fairly obvious at this point that the poem is written in what is called "free verse." In other words, it doesn't rhyme. We'll cover both free verse and rhyming poetry in more detail in Chapter 5.

Other Ways of Getting Started

The above exercise is only one of the ways to getting to grips with the task of starting a poem. There are other things that inspire poetry. I remember once overhearing a news report about something that happened at an airport and the announcer used the phrase, "East of the airport perimeter." I thought it sounded pretty good as the first line of a poem, so that's what I started with and developed a poem about the shadowy world that exists just outside the bounds of civilized society "east of the airport perimeter."

Other ways can also be used. You might start with an image in your mind, which you then describe. Or you might start with a metaphor. I remember coming up with the line, "Fog wandered on the moor like a woman looking for a lost child," and used it as the first line of a sonnet (we'll cover sonnets, later).

I've even taken crossword clues and rearranged them into poetry lines; then tweaked them until they made some kind of sense together. It's amazing how your mind constructs links between completely different phrases and words.

Again, overheard conversations can be good for poem starters, if you can attune your ear to them and pick out the hidden poetic nuggets.

Another way I've used in order to get started is to write down forty or fifty completely unrelated words, verbs, nouns and adjectives, and then play with them. Try putting them together in unusual combinations and see what picture is beginning to emerge. It may just give you a clue as to what you should be writing about and, if your lucky, a first line may emerge from the scattering of phrases you've put down on the page.

Revision

Once you have written a poem, it is important to go back over it and change any parts that look as if they could do with improvement. Of course, you are actually revising the poem as you go along anyway: substituting a word here and there, adjusting the meter, if appropriate, deciding on stanza structure, and so on. But once you have a first draft it can be helpful to set it aside for a while – maybe a day or two, or even a week – and then return to it with fresh eyes. Part of the reason for the delay, is to allow you sufficient time to distance yourself from the poem. While you are writing it, it is very much your own work and you are invested in it. After a gap of a few days, you can come back to it with more detachment. This gives you an opportunity to assess the work critically and enables you to see flaws that you would not otherwise have noticed.

As part of the revision process, one thing that is important to do is to read the poem aloud. You don't need to read it to an audience. The purpose of reading your poem aloud is to make sure that it works properly. There have been a few times I have finished a poem and when I read it aloud I realized that parts of it were almost unpronounceable because they were like tongue twisters! If you identify any elements of your poem that are difficult to read, go back and change them so that they flow more easily.

Another avenue to explore while you are revising the poem is allowing someone else to read it and give you critical comments. This can take a little bit of courage, but it can be worth it if you have someone who is willing to be honest.

Lastly, it can help to return to a batch of poems you have written after several months have passed. Again, the distance makes you more objective about your work and you can identify cracks more clearly. But it also lets you evaluate the poems as a group together. Perhaps you had begun to develop a poetic technique in one poem which you now see could be used for some of the other poems. Or maybe, you touched on a theme with a group of poems which you now see could be expanded into some of the new poems you are now writing. I have even gone back over some previous poems on occasion and realized that they were not as good as I first thought they were, or not as good as the poems I was currently writing, and should therefore not be included as part of the general collection of poems I would put my name to.

Chapter 3 – Other Poetic Techniques

In Chapter 2 we spoke about imagery, where figurative language involving the five senses is used to create an image or impression of a scene in the reader's mind. We covered how simile compares two things using the word "like" or "as", and how metaphor is a word or phrase applied to an object or action to which it is not literally applicable. Here are some other imagery techniques that can be used to good effect to make your poem stand out.

Personification

Personification is a technique whereby you describe an inanimate object as if it were alive. In Dylan Thomas's beautiful poem "Fern Hill," the last stanza ends with the following words:

Oh as I was young and easy in the mercy of his means,
Time held me green and dying
Though I sang in my chains like the sea.

Here he compares himself to the sea which is chained and singing. Obviously, no one can chain the sea, and yet the image rings true; the sea is confined by the land and therefore in a sense it chained like a man in a dungeon. Similarly, the sea is not literally singing, but again the regular sound of the waves and of the tides moving can give the impress of the rhythm of a song.

Alliteration

Alliteration involves repeating the same letter at the beginning of a series of words. Anglo-Saxon poetry relied heavily on alliteration, but there are also plenty of examples of more modern poems that use alliteration to good effect. In the following poem, entitled "Drummore, Scotland," the italicized phrases repeat the letter "b", in order to emphasize the insistent knocking of the boats on the harbor wall at the end of line 8.

A sweep of hill, cramped with gorse and hawthorn,
marks the line of the old road where you see,
fretting by the gate, an ancient turkey;
there are a dozen geese pecking seeds of corn
and a tangled rhododendron blocking
the path to the field and a wizened *briar*
beside the byre's wall obscured by barbed wire
and the harbor boats' insistent knocking.
This is what I remember of Drummore,
its shattered glass of images and sounds,
its unkempt farms and slovenly meadows.
Those were the old days, like an open door
to lives lived by others, their sacred bounds
revealed by all that memories enclose.

Assonance

Assonance takes place when two or more words close to one another repeat the same vowel sound but start with different consonant sounds. Here's an example of how it is used from the second stanza of Edgar Allan Poe's poem "Bells" with the assonant letters underlined:

> Hear the m_e_llow w_e_dding b_e_lls,
> Golden bells!
> What a world of happiness their harmony foretells!
> Through the balmy air of night
> How they ring out their delight!
> From the m_o_lten-g_o_lden n_o_tes,
> And all in tune,
> What a l_i_quid d_i_tty floats
> To the turtle-dove that listens, while she gloats
> On the moon!
> Oh, from out the sounding cells,
> What a gush of euphony voluminously wells!
> How it sw_e_lls!
> How it dw_e_lls

Onomatopoeia

Onomatopoeia is defined as a word, which imitates the natural sounds of a thing. It creates a sound effect that mimics the thing described, making the description more expressive and interesting. Examples are "hiss", "plop", "click", "splash", "crunch", and so on. These can give a much more tactile quality to poetry, especially when combined with alliteration or assonance.

A good example is from the first stanza of the poem we've just mentioned, Edgar Allan Poe's "The Bells."

> HEAR the sledges with the bells,
>> Silver bells!
> What a world of merriment their melody foretells!
>> How they tinkle, tinkle, tinkle,
>>> In the icy air of night!
> While the stars, that oversprinkle
> All the heavens, seem to twinkle
>> With a crystalline delight;
>> Keeping time, time, time,
>>> In a sort of Runic rhyme,
> To the tintinnabulation that so musically wells
>> From the bells, bells, bells, bells,
>>> Bells, bells, bells—
> From the jingling and the tinkling of the bells.

Here, he uses the onomatopoeic words "tinkle", "tintinnabulation", "jingling", and "tinkling" to imitate the sounds that the bells make. These words sound like the thing they are supposed to represent.

Contrast

This technique involves placing two very different images side by side in order to emphasize the qualities of one or the other. In the second last stanza of the following poem, entitled "The Walleye", the fisherman seems to be sympathizing with the fish, with its "unflinching dread / of jeopardy and pain." But then, abruptly, in the last stanza the fisherman kills the walleye and retrieves the hook. This in some sense emphasizes the plight of the fish that is, and has always been, at the mercy of the angler.

> The day I made incision
> in the brass of his lip
> the sun poured down,
> yellow blustering my knees.
>
> The glinting values
> that drove him to the net
> nagged the devil
> out of my eye
>
> till I was blinded.
> He came onto latent peril,
> hiding like a tear duct
> in the shadow of the stern,
>
> and bent an armful of water
> to the momentary strike.
> Languidly he approached, as though
> death were not the matter with him
>
> and sucked down gobs of
> weed and froth and doom
> genteelly like a tea party
> and as thick as my wrist.

His unflinching dread
of jeopardy and pain
were swallowed and digested
with the leeches of the day.

I dashed his brain
on the gunwale
pincered out the hook
and stole the fish away.

Gerard Manley Hopkins also uses contrast in his poem "God's Grandeur," in which he compares the grandeur of God to man's mean lot:

THE WORLD is charged with the grandeur of God.
 It will flame out, like shining from shook foil;
 It gathers to a greatness, like the ooze of oil
Crushed. Why do men then now not reck his rod?
Generations have trod, have trod, have trod;
 And all is seared with trade; bleared, smeared with toil;
 And wears man's smudge and shares man's smell: the soil
Is bare now, nor can foot feel, being shod.

Symbolism

This technique involves making an object stand for something else that is usually abstract. For example, the heart is an organ that pumps blood through the arteries of the body but it can also symbolize love. The rat is an animal but it can also be a symbol of betrayal or underhandedness. A lion is a dangerous animal but it can also be a symbol of courage.

Hyperbole

Hyperbole is a form of exaggeration – as in the phrase, "I've told you a million times not to exaggerate." William Wordsword uses hyperbole twice in the second stanza of his poem "The Daffodils."

> Continuous as the stars that shine
> And twinkle on the milky way,
> They stretched in never-ending line
> Along the margin of a bay:
> Ten thousand saw I at a glance,
> Tossing their heads in sprightly dance.

The line of daffodils is not really never-ending, and it seems unlikely that there are ten thousand of them. Nevertheless the hyperbole is effective since it gives the impression of a huge number of flowers stretching into the distance.

Hyperbole can also add humor – "he had a butt like a hippopotamus and a personality to match" or emphasize the strength of a person's feelings – "football isn't just a matter of life and death; it's more important than that". However, you have to be careful with hyperbole because if it is overused it ceases to be effective.

Repetition

The repetition of words or phrases in a poem can set up a steady or insistent rhythm as the poem progresses or can intensify the feeling the poet is trying to convey. In this poem from Alfred, Lord Tennyson, called "Tears, Idle Tears," the impression of grief is heightened by the repetition of the phrase, "the days that are no more," at the end of each stanza.

> Tears, idle tears, I know not what they mean,
> Tears from the depth of some divine despair
> Rise in the heart, and gather to the eyes,
> In looking on the happy Autumn-fields,
> And thinking of the days that are no more.
>
> Fresh as the first beam glittering on a sail,
> That brings our friends up from the underworld,
> Sad as the last which reddens over one
> That sinks with all we love below the verge;
> So sad, so fresh, the days that are no more.
>
> Ah, sad and strange as in dark summer dawns
> The earliest pipe of half-awaken'd birds
> To dying ears, when unto dying eyes
> The casement slowly grows a glimmering square;
> So sad, so strange, the days that are no more.
>
> Dear as remember'd kisses after death,
> And sweet as those by hopeless fancy feign'd
> On lips that are for others; deep as love,

Deep as first love, and wild with all regret;
O Death in Life, the days that are no more!

Using Poetic Techniques

These are some of the main techniques that are useful for writing poetry. By now it will have become clear that producing good poetry relies not only on writing words that are sincere, but also on shrewdly using the techniques available to you.

Obviously, not all of these methods will be used with every poem, but it is helpful to be aware of what is at hand. The more you practice using the various skills here the more easily you can produce good poetry confidently and the more natural it becomes.

Chapter 4 – How to Produce a Good Poem

There is a lot of poetry in the world and a lot of it is not very good. One of the reasons for that is that most people seem to think that in order to write a good poem the main qualification is that it has to be sincere. Whatever your reason for writing a poem, you owe it to yourself, if not to others, to produce the best work you can. It is true that anyone can write a poem, but writing a *good* poem involves a number of qualities other than sincerity: sensitivity to the language, avoiding clichés, practice, imagination, being open to criticism, and even courage.

Sensitivity to Language

One of the things that helps in the writing of poetry is reading other people's poetry, especially the poetry of good poets. The reason why we benefit from reading other poetry is that gradually we become more and more attuned the rhythm of the language, how other poets have chosen which words to use, how they have rhymed the ends of the lines in a poem, how they have used metaphor and simile. It gradually builds a feeling within us of what is possible in a poem. It gives us a sense of how powerful poetry can be and an inkling of how to achieve the same effects.

Avoiding Clichés

One thing to say about using metaphors and similes

is that you can run the risk of trotting out the usual stock phrases everyone uses. You know, the tired old clichés such as: "her brow was cold as ice"; "he was as hard as nails"; "as stealthy as a cat," and so on.

These kinds of phrases make your poetry dull and powerless. So it is worth looking for unusual combinations like: "her brow was cold as a marble plinth"; "he was as hard as a granite dolmen"; "as stealthy as the creeping dawn," and so on.

Practice

Another way in which we can gain skill at writing poetry is... by writing it! Producing good poetry takes a degree of skill. As with any craft or art form, the more you practice the better you get at it. It's as simple as that. Often poetry is not just the effusion of emotion that people seem to think it is. Poetry takes work, if it is to be any good. Who can tell how many genuinely "sincere" poems have been produced which, nevertheless, are not well written because they were a one-off and because the writer lacked the skill that comes from practice.

It's true that poetry can be used to express powerful emotions. But how well those emotions are expressed is often in direct proportion, not to the overwhelming feelings of the poet, but to the degree to which the author practiced his art.

When I first started writing poetry something that helped me progress was that I came to view all my efforts as merely practice. This was tremendously useful. It meant that the pressure was off. I could make mistakes and learn the craft of writing poetry until I could consider myself good enough to present my poems not to an imaginary audience but a real one.

When you come to write a poem, it is always useful to have a particular place to write where you won't be disturbed. Writing poetry takes concentration, so minimize as many distractions as possible. Also choose a time when you are alert. This varies for different people. Some people are sleepier in the morning, others in the afternoon, and so on.

I believe that, if you are serious about writing poetry, it is crucial to master the techniques of poetry writing, including rhyme and meter, so that when the time comes and you are inspired to write on a particular subject you have all the tools and mental equipment needed to carry out the task to the best of your ability. That also means writing regularly, not just when the mood strikes you. It doesn't mean you have to write a poem every day. But one poem a week might not be beyond the bounds of possibility.

Imagination

It's true that the degree to which you are imaginative or creative is not entirely under your control. But there are things that can help even the most modest level of creativity to produce good poetry. We covered some of those ways in Chapter 2. However, what helps a great deal is if you can develop a good ear and listen to what other people say, how they use language, how they combine words. Listen to the rhythms of everyday speech and learn from them.

Be Open to Criticism

Another tool in the toolbox of learning to write poetry is having someone who will give you a balanced opinion on how good it is, or make suggestions that might improve a particular poem. It's not a matter of closing your eyes and screwing up your face and asking someone to tell you what's wrong with your poem. There may be nothing wrong with it. It's a case of asking someone who has some skill at discerning good poetry from bad poetry to tell you what works and what doesn't. If you're open enough and want to improve, this kind of constructive criticism can be of great benefit. This is covered more fully in Chapter 9.

Courage

Poetry is a form of shorthand. By the use of imagery you can suggest much more complex impressions and convey feelings and information in a more condensed form than you can with prose. So as part of your review process, once you have written the poem, go back over what you have written to see if there are any words that are superfluous. If there are words that don't really contribute anything to the sense you are trying to get across and they won't be missed, cut them out. It takes courage to slash through the work you've spent ages working on, but believe me it is almost always the case that less is more.

Saying More than You Say

Good poems describe an object, person, event, or anecdote, but also extrapolate that into some universal truth or point out some wider implication. It is not enough simply to tell a story about how a child got lost in a shopping mall. What elevates a poem beyond mere facts or descriptions, is if you can step back and perhaps make some more general statement about the fragility of life, or compare our own lot in life to that of the child.

However, you have to be careful that you don't simply make the general comment explicit at the end of the poem, but rather hint or refer to it obliquely, or weave it into the fabric of the poem itself. You also need to be careful about using clichéd phrases if you are going to make a wider comment on life. And it is easy to fall into the trap of becoming sentimental. Subtlety and power, originality and weight are what you should be aiming at.

Poetry Journal

If you are fairly serious about writing poetry it is a good idea to keep a poetry journal, where you can record poetry ideas and drafts of poems you are working on or have finished. Another way of achieving the same thing is by having a folder on your computer for poems. This has the added advantage that you can back up your files onto separate media – for example, a flash drive – and can also password-protect your work so that no one else can casually browse through your poems. I find it useful to include the title and date with any poems I write so that I can see what progress I have made over time.

Chapter 5 – Free Verse or Formal Verse

Many people prefer free verse (that is unrhymed poetry) to formal verse (which is not, as it sounds, poetry that is stuffy, prim and proper but simply poetry which uses "form", including rhyme and meter). Rhymed verse, it is thought, seems somehow artificial or contrived and can't really express the true feelings of the writer. Free verse, on the other hand, liberates you to give full reign to your emotions and put down whatever comes into your head without having to bother with meter or rhyme.

Comparing the Two

However there are many poems that express deeply-felt emotions but follow the strict rules of formal poetry. One example is Ben Jonson's poem "On My First Sonne." It is an incredibly touching poem set down in rhyming couplets – lines which rhyme in pairs – which you would not have thought at all suited to powerful emotion. It was written on the death of his little son, on the child's seventh birthday. The little boy was named Benjamin after his father, and Benjamin means "child of my right hand" hence the opening line. There are three short verses.

Farewell, thou child of my right hand, and joy;
My sin was too much hope of thee, lov'd boy.
Seven years thou wert lent to me, and I thee pay,
Exacted by thy fate, on the just day.

Oh, could I lose all father now! For why
Will man lament the state he should envy?
To have so soon 'scaped world's and flesh's rage,
And if no other misery, yet age!

Rest in soft peace, and, asked, say, Here doth lie
Ben Jonson his best piece of poetry.
For whose sake henceforth all his vows be such
As what he loves may never like too much.

See what I mean? With poetry, sometimes, if you want to express deep emotion in a beautiful way, the discipline of meter and rhyme can be much more effective than the apparent rambling nature of free verse, because of its potential dignity and the opportunities it affords for setting up a rhythm within the language.

However, one of the reasons why many people prefer free verse to formal poetry is because it seems easier to write. It's true that free verse does not involve you in the intricacies of having to count out the beats in each line and making sure each line rhymes with its corresponding line. But to a certain extent, without the crutch of form, free verse is naked. Without using rhyme and meter, free verse has to stand on its own two feet and be good enough to withstand the scrutiny of the reader without caving in after the first few lines.

Formal poetry has the other advantage that when you are using meter, that is a strict set of beats or syllables in each line, it forces you to use word order and word choice which does not necessarily correspond to the way people speak or even the way they write prose. For example, one of the most common meters in English poetry is "iambic pentameter" (we'll cover it in more detail in Chapter 6 on sonnets) which requires ten syllables in each line alternating short and long stresses. The fact is, in normal speech, people don't talk in iambic pentameter. So the fact that you have to make the words of your poem fit that pattern immediately makes a poem sound more, well, poetic.

On the other hand, free verse does not necessarily have to be formless either. A free verse poem may be divided into stanzas. Quite often the stanzas of a free-verse poem can be regular – for example, they may all be three lines long. Similarly, where each line ends may not necessarily be as arbitrary as it seems. Here is a free verse poem, entitled "Moss", that demonstrates this.

> The simple scrap of moss
> on this stone is livid,
> outshining its solemner rivals.
> It grows on nothing,
> taking sustenance from the air
> in a concentrated unison
> of organic particles.
>
> Imitating the complexity
> of larger plants,
> whose plain jackets
> of Lincoln green and brown
> impress this corner
> of the garden with bright life,

the tuft's slow sinews glow.

Should I extirpate
with a swift movement
of hand or foot
this growing thing,
or leave it to its
wild green age
of muted fire?

How many of my own
small hesitant growths
are like this moss,
hidden and unnoticed
by a corner of life,
hooked with careful nature
to some rock or plank?

I rub it with a coarse finger
and it springs back.
I tug lightly the stem
between finger and thumb,
but I will not kill it after all,
nor snub out my own life
by the desecration.

All creatures have their time
and we are fellows
for as long as we live
in the shadow of the sun.
And perhaps someone else

looks gladly down
and stays his hand for me.

Here, each stanza is seven lines long and the lines break naturally after each unit of meaning – a unit of meaning being a phrase that has either a noun or a verb, or both. With free verse, it's not necessary to include these elements of form, like regular stanzas and logical line breaks, but it is possible.

If we go back to Ben Jonson's poem about his dead son, we also notice that each line is made up of ten syllables – except the third line in the first verse, which has twelve syllables:

Seven years thou wert lent to me, and I thee pay,

Perhaps the poet made that line longer to indicate time passing. In any case, Jonson's poem demonstrates that, even if you are following the seemingly strict rules of formal poetry, those rules can be bent or even broken if you have a good reason to break or bend them. Similarly, with free verse you can include elements of form if it seems appropriate. So in actual fact between formal verse and free verse there is something of a continuum, one blending into the other.

If you are just starting out to write poetry more or less from scratch, free verse is certainly easier to write. But as you get more used to writing poetry it is good to take on the challenge of writing some formal poems. You may be pleasantly surprised at how it changes the types of words you use and makes your work sound more dynamic!

By the way, if you are going to write rhymed poetry you may find it useful to consult a rhyming dictionary. You can find rhyming dictionaries online, too, which allow you to enter a word and then give you a list of other words that rhyme with it. But be careful you don't rely on it too much, or it may stifle creativity.

Rhymes and Slant-rhymes

Choose which words you want to rhyme carefully. Some words don't really rhyme with many other words, for example knife only rhymes directly with fife, life, rife, strife and wife, which doesn't give you much scope for expanding the meaning of your poem, and orange strictly doesn't rhyme with anything, so some words are best avoided. You can use a rhyming dictionary to check how many words rhyme with the one you have placed at the end of your line of poetry.

One way round the problem of making a poem rhyme exactly is using what are called off-rhymes or slant-rhymes. Slant-rhymes are words that don't rhyme strictly but sound similar. The following poem uses slant-rhymes in several places:

> Suspended above the city, in the last
> anxiety of cloud and coming rain,
> the voices become thick with tears, the pain
> calling for quarter as the night passes
> outward towards the split ends of the line.
> Strung out between the poles are the bodies

of fellow travelers, still moving, copies
of each other in their capricious time.
Bareback streets and barren houses dissolve
into the steam on the windows, rattling
towards Epping, and inside we are one
great, black jolting can of worms, who devolve
into worm casts as the train moves, battling
wayfarers, jostled and startled in turn.

In the above poem "passes" in line 4 is used to slant-rhyme with "last" in line 1; "line" slant-rhymes with "time"; "bodies" with "copies"; and "one" with "turn." Slant-rhymes offer the poet much more scope for developing the narrative or argument of the poem without having to spend a whole lot of time searching for the right word to rhyme strictly with the one at the end of his or her line, or bending the meaning of the poem round to fit the rhymes.

Line Length

As mentioned, where we end a line can be a useful device that adds to the meaning of the poem or reinforces the effect we are trying to achieve. Take the following lines:

The climber turned,
Fiddling with his harness and
Dropped into the merciless abyss

Most people, when reading poetry, pause slightly at the end of each line – especially if each line constitutes a unit of meaning like a phrase or sentence. So these lines could actually be improved by moving the "dropped" in line three to the end of line two, thus:

The climber turned,
Fiddling with his harness, and dropped
Into the merciless abyss

There is a slight pause after the word "dropped" which gives it added dramatic impact. With strict formal poetry there is less scope for deciding where to end a line, since the meter usually decides that for you. But in free verse, it is worth playing around with word order and positioning to see if you can enhance an effect by taking advantage of that unwritten pause at the end of each line.

Chapter 6 – The Sonnet

The sonnet has been around for centuries and for centuries it has been used as the key form for love poetry. A sonnet is a poetic form that originated in Italy. The term sonnet is derived from the Italian word *sonetto*, which means little song. By the thirteenth century it signified a poem of fourteen lines that follows a strict rhyme scheme and specific structure. Conventions associated with the sonnet have evolved over its history.

Rhyme Scheme

One of the best-known sonnet writers is William Shakespeare, who wrote 154 sonnets. A Shakespearean or English sonnet consists of fourteen lines written in iambic pentameter (see below). The rhyme scheme in a Shakespearean sonnet is a-b-a-b, c-d-c-d, e-f-e-f, g-g. This notation, a-b-a-b for example, simply means that line one (a) rhymes with line three (which is also a), and line two (b) rhymes with line four (which is also b) and so on. The last two lines, g-g, form what is called a rhyming couplet, i.e. two lines placed together which rhyme with each other.

Here is an example of one of Shakespeare's sonnets:

Shall I compare thee to a summer's day? (a)
Thou art more lovely and more temperate: (b)
Rough winds do shake the darling buds of May, (a)

And summer's lease hath all too short a date; (b)
Sometime too hot the eye of heaven shines, (c)
And often is his gold complexion dimm'd; (d)
And every fair from fair sometime declines, (c)
By chance or nature's changing course untrimm'd; (d)
But thy eternal summer shall not fade, (e)
Nor lose possession of that fair thou ow'st; (f)
Nor shall Death brag thou wander'st in his shade, (e)
When in eternal lines to time thou grow'st: (f)
So long as men can breathe or eyes can see, (g)
So long lives this, and this gives life to thee. (g)

Iambic Pentameter

A Shakespearean or English sonnet consists of fourteen lines written in iambic pentameter, a pattern in which an unstressed syllable is followed by a stressed syllable five times, thus making ten syllables per line. The word "pentameter" means "having five metrical parts". So there are five elements in a pentameter. The word "iambic" describes what each of those elements contains. An iamb is a short, or unstressed, syllable followed by a long, or stressed, syllable

To make it easier to understand, an iambic pentameter line sounds like this:

De-dah | de-dah | de-dah | de-dah | de-dah

Shall I | compare | thee to | a sum | mer's day?

It can be a bit tricky getting the hang of iambic pentameter. In fact, many modern poets simply opt for having ten syllables per line rather than making them strictly iambic.

Other Rhyme Schemes

The two most common rhyme schemes for the sonnet are: the Shakespearean sonnet (a-b-a-b, c-d-c-d, e-f-e-f, g-g) and the Petrarchan sonnet (a-b-b-a, a-b-b-a, c-d-e, c-d-e), which is used in John Milton's poem, "On His Blindness."

When I consider how my light is spent
Ere half my days, in this dark world and wide,
And that one talent which is death to hide,
Lodged with me useless, though my soul more bent
To serve therewith my Maker, and present
My true account, lest he returning chide;
"Doth God exact day-labor, light denied?"
I fondly ask; but Patience to prevent
That murmur, soon replies, "God doth not need
Either man's work or his own gifts; who best
Bear his mild yoke, they serve him best. His state
Is Kingly. Thousands at his bidding speed
And post o'er land and ocean without rest;
They also serve who only stand and wait."

Nevertheless, modern sonnets can take on many variations on the basic forms, such as a-b-b-a, c-d-d-c, e-f-g, e-f-g, which is used in the following sonnet called "Fourteen Afternoons."

That afternoon, faint words and background noise
broke over me upon awakening
in the ward. Coming out of darkening
woods under the starlight that dawn destroys,
the long journey back from unconsciousness
took time, and time was heavy on my mind.
Two weeks of boyhood for the wound to bind.
Till then it would be rest and rootlessness.
There would be a scar (the operation
back then was never keyhole surgery).
Now, instead I seek keys to other wounds
that have lasted longer than the ration
of a casual appendectomy.
They are not cured in fourteen afternoons.

Notice that the above poem does not keep strictly to iambic pentameter, but does adhere to the rule that there should be ten syllables per line. So there is a degree of leeway for modern sonnets that was less prominent in the past. This poem also exhibits two techniques: **enjambment** and **caesura**. An enjambment is when a sentence or phrase does not end at the end of a line but carries on to the next line as is the case with the first two lines of the poem: "That afternoon, faint words and background noise / broke over me." A caesura is when a sentence finishes somewhere in the middle of a line, as is the case with the third line: "in the ward. Coming out of darkness…"

Subject Matter

As mentioned there has been a tradition in English and European poetry of the past to use the sonnet to express love for another person. But, as you can see with two of the above examples, the sonnet can be pressed into service to cover virtually any subject at all. As with other forms of poetry, the more practice you get at sonnet writing the better you become.

Sonnet Walkthrough

Let's attempt a walkthrough of a sonnet using one of the rhyme schemes associated with the sonnet (a-b-b-a, c-d-d-c, e-f-g, e-f-g), and with the correct meter and number of lines. First, the subject. What about something unusual? City vermin: rats. First we'll set the scene. It's winter and there are piles of snow about the place. So what about:

The long nights that lurk around the streets

But that's only nine syllables and it's not entirely iambic. Let's try inserting "and fevered" after the word "long."

The long and fevered nights that lurk around
the streets

Now the first line scans correctly in iambic pentameter but it's pushed the last two words onto line two. That's okay. We'll try to add to it:

> *The long and fevered nights that lurk around*
> *the streets in winter glow with hulking heaps*
> *of dirty snow.*

Just to make the rhythm clear we'll underline the strongly stressed syllables and divide the lines up into iambs, so we can see that it works according to the sonnet rules. Remember an iamb is a weak, or unstressed, syllable followed by a strong, or stressed syllable.

> *The <u>long</u> | and <u>fe</u> | vered <u>nights</u> | that <u>lurk</u> a | <u>round</u>*
> *the <u>streets</u> | in <u>win</u> | ter <u>glow</u> | with <u>hul</u> | king <u>heaps</u>*
> *of <u>dir</u> | ty <u>snow</u>.*

So far so good. We have two and a bit lines and they are in iambic pentameter. Whatever we add to "dirty snow" the line has to rhyme with the end of line two: "heaps." What about "leaps?" Well rats don't often manage those kinds of acrobatics and, besides, "leaps" has more positive connotations than we want to get across. "Keeps?" Sleeps?" "Creeps?" Yes, what about "creeps"; that fits in well with rodents. We also have to get line four to rhyme with line one.

So let's finish off the a-b-b-a lines:

> *The long and fevered nights that lurk around*
> *the streets in winter glow with hulking heaps*

of dirty snow. And through the silence creeps
the stealthy urban beast that makes no sound.

If you read this aloud, you can detect the iambic rhythm to the poem. Also, you'll notice that we are not stopping sentences at the end of a line (except at the end of line four), but rather letting the sentence run on to the next line using both **enjambment** and **caesura**.

Only ten lines to go. We want to say something about how rats skulk invisibly in the background. Here are the next few lines:

All through the blinding days of sun and snow
and through the delicate and dreary dark
the unseen citizens of suburbs mark
their country, leaving us no place to go.

We're into a rhythm now and the iambic pentameter begins to get easier. As you're writing the poem, though, you have to be aware of the fact that you're going to have to come up with a rhyme at the end of each line, and keep track of what the last word should rhyme with. In order to do that you have to think ahead and mold what you're saying round the rhyme at the end. You can see that when writing formal poetry like this you can't just write down whatever comes into your head, but must constantly be aware of the form.

Normally, with this rhyme scheme the sonnet should be divided into two parts. In the first eight lines you make a proposal or describe a scene or lay down an argument. Then in the last six lines you change tack and begin to draw some conclusions. In a sense, this form of sonnet is like two poems bolted together.

So what do we want to say in the last six lines? That we share our cities with an unseen interloper – the rat – with a bit of give-and-take on either side.

Here are the next three lines of the e-f-g, e-f-g conclusion.

> *That other geography in every town*
> *obtains its purchase in the dreamless night*
> *and taints the trash to which we give our name.*

In other words rats have a different geography than we do for getting round the city at night, part of which involves landmarks like trashcans. Now we need a concluding three lines which rhyme correctly to e-f-g.

> *Our cherished property is not our own.*
> *We share it with that shadowland and fight*
> *among ourselves and thus we play the game.*

So here's the full sonnet:

The long and fevered nights that lurk around
the streets in winter glow with hulking heaps
of dirty snow. And through the silence creeps
the stealthy urban beast that makes no sound.
All through the blinding days of sun and snow
and through the delicate and dreary dark
the unseen citizens of suburbs mark
their country, leaving us no place to go.

That other geography in every town
obtains its purchase in the dreamless night
and taints the trash to which we give our name.
Our cherished property is not our own.
We share it with that shadowland and fight
among ourselves and thus we play the game.

A respectable attempt at this genre and worth the effort. Like any other form of craft, writing rhyming poetry and iambic pentameter takes a little practice. But once you've got the hang of it, like riding a bike, you never forget how it's done.

The Sonnet Game

If you have one or two friends who enjoy writing poetry, here's an exercise that can be a lot of fun to do together. It's called the Sonnet Game and the purpose is to write a number of sonnets.

First of all, you decide together what rhyme scheme will be used for the game, say a-b-a-b, c-d-c-d, e-f-e-f, g-g. Each player starts off with a blank sheet of paper and writes down the first line of a sonnet in iambic pentameter. Each player then passes the sheet clockwise. Now each player has a sheet with the first line on it (written by the previous person). They now write the second line of the poem in front of them, always keeping to the rhyme scheme that has been agreed and pass the sheet clockwise again. The sheets are passed round until fourteen lines of each sonnet have been completed. Each player gives a title to the poem in front of him or her and you each take turns at reading out the resulting sonnets.

Usually the results are hilarious. But, as well as being entertaining, it is also very good practice at writing sonnets and is excellent practice for reading poetry aloud.

Chapter 7 – Odes, Ballads, Haikus & Love Poems

Apart from the sonnet, there are other forms of poetry that have been used for years in various different situations and for different types of events. Here are four of the most popular: the ode, the ballad, the haiku and the love poem.

The Ode

Traditionally, an ode is structured in three major parts: the *strophe*, the *antistrophe*, and the *epode*. The first part puts forward an argument or proposal; the second counters it; and the third brings about a resolution of the two. It is an elaborately structured poem praising or glorifying an event or individual, describing nature intellectually as well as emotionally. It is a formal address to a person or thing that is not present. It can be used for special occasions and doesn't have to be long. Modern odes don't necessarily keep to the traditional form, but are still characterized as addressing an individual or object. All sorts of poets have tried their hand at the ode over the years but it was a particularly favorite form of the Romantic poets, Coleridge, Keats and Shelley. Keats's "Ode to Autumn" is a good example:

Season of mists and mellow fruitfulness

Close bosom-friend of the maturing sun
Conspiring with him how to load and bless
With fruit the vines that round the thatch-eaves run;
To bend with apples the moss'd cottage-trees,
And fill all fruit with ripeness to the core;
To swell the gourd, and plump the hazel shells
With a sweet kernel; to set budding more,
And still more, later flowers for the bees,
Until they think warm days will never cease,
For Summer has o'er-brimm'd their clammy cells.

Who hath not seen thee oft amid thy store?
Sometimes whoever seeks abroad may find
Thee sitting careless on a granary floor,
Thy hair soft-lifted by the winnowing wind;
Or on a half-reap'd furrow sound asleep,
Drows'd with the fume of poppies, while thy hook
Spares the next swath and all its twined flowers:
And sometimes like a gleaner thou dost keep
Steady thy laden head across a brook;
Or by a cider-press, with patient look,
Thou watchest the last oozings hours by hours.

Where are the songs of Spring? Ay, where are they?
Think not of them, thou hast thy music too,-
While barred clouds bloom the soft-dying day,
And touch the stubble-plains with rosy hue;
Then in a wailful choir the small gnats mourn
Among the river sallows, borne aloft
Or sinking as the light wind lives or dies;
And full-grown lambs loud bleat from hilly bourn;

Hedge-crickets sing; and now with treble soft
The red-breast whistles from a garden-croft;
And gathering swallows twitter in the skies.

The poem has three stanzas in praise of autumn. Each of the stanzas has eleven lines and each line has ten syllables, which may or may not be iambic. You can see that in the second stanza Keats employs personification to conjure up the image of autumn "sitting careless on a granary floor, / Thy hair soft-lifted by the winnowing wind." He also uses assonance in the last line of that stanza as he describes the "oozings hours by hours." In the poem he describes in three stanzas early autumn, the middle point of the season, and the beginning signs of approaching winter.

As I mentioned, you can use the ode on special occasions, such as somebody's birthday, or a wedding, an anniversary or any other event in which you can direct your poem towards a person or thing.

The Ballad

A ballad is a form of verse, which is often a narrative. Originally ballads were set to music. In fact, the word "ballad" comes from the French word to dance. So they were originally dancing songs. There are three distinct types of ballads:

Traditional British ballads. These can be humorous, tragic, or even satirical, and are often on themes such as death, love, and work.

British broadsides. (A broadside was a sheet of paper on which a ballad was printed and which used to be sold in the streets by peddlers in earlier centuries). These tend to be on current events of the day and may have a political bent. They tend to be an opportunity for the poet to rant about some injustice that has happened to him or complain about general conditions in society.

North American ballads. These also deal with love, scandal, violence, and disaster. These were sung by particular groups, for example, miners, sailors, or cowboys. Classic North American ballads include "John Henry" and "Casey Jones."

However, they have evolved over the years and most poetic ballads are now medium to long narrative poems, which are ideal for reading aloud or even being sung to accompaniment.

Ballads are very often written in rhyming couplets (i.e. a-a, b-b, c-c and so on) and have a regular meter, which may or may not be iambic. And there may be a refrain after every couplet or group of couplets.

If you want to write a ballad, the first thing you have to do is to come up with a subject and a storyline. There is no point in starting writing unless you know ultimately where you're going. There's little room for rambling with a ballad; you don't want to bore the audience. The main thing you want to do is to get into a rhythm so that the poem takes on a pace of its own. Then just follow the story through to the end.

As with any other work of poetry, once you have completed a first draft, it pays to go over what you've written and make sure that it scans properly (i.e. that the rhythm doesn't falter in places). Depending on what type of ballad you are writing, the opportunities for humor are endless. Here's a sample from the start of a traditional Scottish ballad called Sir Patrick Spens by an unknown author:

The King sits in Dunfermline town,
Drinking the blood-red wine;
"O where shall I get a skeely skipper
To sail this ship or mine?"

Then up and spake an eldern knight,
Sat at the King's right knee:
"Sir Patrick Spens is the best sailor
That ever sailed the sea."

The King has written a broad letter,
And sealed it with his hand,
And sent it to Sir Patrick Spens,
Was walking on the strand.

"To Noroway, to Noroway,
To Noroway o'er the foam;
The King's daughter of Noroway,
'Tis thou must fetch her home."

The first line that Sir Patrick read,
A loud laugh laughéd he;
The next line that Sir Patrick read,
The tear blinded his ee.

"O who is this has done this deed,
Has told the King of me,
To send us out at this time of the year,
To sail upon the sea?

Here's part of the North American ballad, "John Henry," which is also by an anonymous author:

When John Henry was a little tiny baby
Sitting on his mama's knee,
He picked up a hammer and a little piece of steel
Saying, "Hammer's going to be the death of me, Lord, Lord,
    Hammer's going to be the death of me."

John Henry was a man just six feet high,
Nearly two feet and a half across his breast.
He'd hammer with a nine-pound hammer all day
And never get tired and want to rest, Lord, Lord,
    And never get tired and want to rest.

John Henry went up on the mountain
And he looked one eye straight up its side.
The mountain was so tall and John Henry was so small,
He laid down his hammer and he cried, "Lord, Lord,"
    He laid down his hammer and he cried.

John Henry said to his captain,
"Captain, you go to town,
Bring me back a twelve-pound hammer, please,
And I'll beat that steam drill down, Lord, Lord,
    I'll beat that steam drill down."

The captain said to John Henry,
"I believe this mountain's sinking in."
But John Henry said, "Captain, just you stand aside--
It's nothing but my hammer catching wind, Lord, Lord,
　It's nothing but my hammer catching wind."

John Henry said to his shaker,
"Shaker, boy, you better start to pray,
'Cause if my twelve-pound hammer miss that little piece of steel,
Tomorrow'll be your burying day, Lord, Lord,
　Tomorrow'll be your burying day."

The Haiku

　　　The haiku is a form of poetry that originated in Japan. Haikus are typically short and pithy and are quite often based round an emotional experience or a scene from nature or an object of great beauty. The typical structure of a haiku is that it should contain 17 syllables (or *on* in Japanese). The syllables arrange themselves as 5-7-5 on three lines. On the other hand, modern English haikus can contain more than 17 syllables or less; the rule is not strictly adhered to. But if you decide to write a haiku the Japanese tradition is that a haiku should be able to be read in one breath.

　　　The essence of the haiku is to put two different images together, usually augmented by a *kigo*, which is a word or short phrase that refers to the time in which the poem is set – for example, spring, winter, night, dawn,

Independence Day. Each phrase should be taken from a different image and by putting them together the whole is greater than the sum of the parts. In other words, each image enhances the other.

The first stage in writing a haiku is deciding what the subject is. You might choose something from nature, say insects crawling on leaves. The second image may look at the same scene from a totally different perspective, for example mentioning the way a wood is bordered by a river. So you might end up with this:

Beetles crawl on leaves.
The deep golden wood is bound
by shouting waters.

Just as in any other poem, with the haiku you have to use your five senses. What do you see, hear, taste, touch and smell? Similarly, you don't have to make the *kiro*, the time word or phrase, obvious. In the above haiku, the word "golden" indicates that the scene takes place in the fall. And, as always, avoid clichés: "an apple never falls far from the tree," "as fresh as a daisy," "between a rock and a hard place," etc. Here we have used the word "shouting" to describe the waters rather than the more hackneyed "raging."

It's worth reading other people's haikus to get an idea of how they work. It is also very useful to take inspiration from the world around you. Carrying a notebook with you, in which you can jot down ideas, is helpful. You might be inspired by anything as disparate as a cat rummaging through a trashcan, or a sunset behind an apartment block, a flower growing through a crack in the sidewalk, or a distant mountaintop wreathed in mist.

Here are some examples of haikus from probably the most famous Japanese exponent, Matsu Bashō:

With dewdrops dripping,
I wish somehow I could wash
this perishing world

where's the moon?
as the temple bell is --
sunk in the sea

The moon about to appear,
all present tonight
with their hands on their knees.

autumn winds
in the sliding door's opening
a sharp voice

low tide morning...
the willow skirts are tailed
in stinking mud

borrowing sleep
from the scarecrow's sleeves
midnight frost

Buddha's Death Day
from wrinkled praying hands

the rosaries' sound

so clear the sound
echoes to the Big Dipper
the fulling block

The Love Poem

Probably one of the most common genres of poetry that people want to write is the love poem. There can be no more personal and endearing gift to give your soul mate than to write a poem specifically for him or her. And it can be so much more meaningful than using someone else's poem, don't you think?

Once again, the more practice you have at writing poetry, the greater the chances of your love poem being effective. As we observed before, people often think it's enough to be sincere in what you write for it to be acceptable. In truth, that *is* quite often the case with love poetry. The mere fact of the poem's existence is proof enough of your love. But if you want it to be something that your loved one cherishes and returns to again and again over the years, then why not make the effort of producing a good poem. The same rules to achieve a good poem apply here, as they did in Chapter 4. And you can use the same steps outlined in Chapters 2 and 3, where you use the five senses and the various poetic techniques to give your poem maximum impact.

Nevertheless, what proves most useful is, before you begin, if you can write down one or two sentence that sum up what you want to get across in the poem. That way you can keep track of whether you poem is achieving your goal as you go along.

One of the traditional forms used for love poetry is the sonnet (see Chapter 6), but any style of poem can be used from formal poetry to free verse. Here are some examples. First, one from Emily Dickenson, called "Wild Nights" in which only the second and fourth lines in each stanza rhyme.

Wild nights! Wild nights!
Were I with thee,
Wild nights should be
Our luxury!

Futile the winds
To a heart in port,
Done with the compass,
Done with the chart.

Rowing in Eden!
Ah! the sea!
Might I but moor
To-night in thee!

In the following short poem by the Irish poet W.B. Yeats, it is slightly ambiguous whether he is praising his sweetheart or his bottle of wine!

Wine comes in at the mouth
And love comes in at the eye;

That's all we shall know for truth
Before we grow old and die.
I lift the glass to my mouth,
I look at you, and I sigh.

Now, a famous sonnet by Elizabeth Barrett Browning. She married the poet Robert Browning against her father's wishes and they eloped to Italy. So, despite her Victorian upbringing she was certainly well acquainted with heady romance.

How do I love thee? Let me count the ways.
I love thee to the depth and breadth and height
My soul can reach, when feeling out of sight
For the ends of Being and ideal Grace.
I love thee to the level of everyday's
Most quiet need, by sun and candle-light.
I love thee freely, as men strive for Right;
I love thee purely, as they turn from Praise.
I love thee with a passion put to use
In my old griefs, and with my childhood's faith.
I love thee with a love I seemed to lose
With my lost saints, — I love thee with the breath,
Smiles, tears, of all my life! — and, if God choose,
I shall but love thee better after death.

There are many different sentiments that can be expressed in a love poem. But it is obvious from the above selection that each poem actually says something. None of them is simply an artless gushing forth of emotion. There is a sense of emotion, true, but it is under the control of poetic technique, and that makes each of these poems all the more effective in its own right.

One thing to say about love poetry is that, although a good poem shouldn't be just an effusion of unbridled feelings, if you want the message of love to the loved one to get through, it should, in fact, be sincere. Good love poems tend to be less flowery nowadays than they were in the past, but there is still a lot of room for schmaltz, if you feel the inclination. It's a delicate balance, though, between authenticity and technique, which is why the more practice you get at writing other types of poems, the more you will be ready to write a love poem. It's worth tackling for the challenge of expressing something which is very important to you – and, hopefully, to the recipient!

Chapter 8 – Humorous Poetry

There is no better way to mark a special occasion than to write and perform a poem to commemorate it. And quite often this gives us room for humor. Conversely, you might just feel like writing a witty ditty just for fun. For whatever reason, the resulting poem is always much more effective if it is written well. Usually the best form of verse for humorous poetry is rhymed and metered and when it is being performed emphasis is quite often placed on getting into the rhythm of the poem.

Cautionary Tales

With narrative humorous poems, the subject may be anything, and the same guidelines apply to humorous poetry that apply to more serious works. Here are three short poems by Harry Graham, which are funny in a macabre kind of way:

> Weep not for little Leonie,
> Abducted by a French Marquis!
> Though loss of honor was a wrench,
> Just think how it's improved her French.

> Billy, in one of his nice new sashes
> Fell in the fire and was burnt to ashes
> And now, although the room grows chilly,
> I haven't the heart to poke poor Billy.

Nurse, who peppered baby's face
(She mistook it for a muffin),
Held her tongue and kept her place,
'Laying low and sayin' nuffin';
Mother, seeing baby blinded,
Said, "Oh, nurse, how absent-minded!"

G.K. Chesterton was a master of humorous poetry too. Here's an example of one of his poems:

Of Uncle Humphrey who can sing?
His name can't rhyme with anything,
How much superior is Aunt Harriet
Who rhymes correctly to Iscariot

But humorous poems can, of course, be longer. Here's one entitled "The Inadvisability of Rotten Eggs":

The egg is tasty, rather good;
A very reasonable food.
But what becomes of yellow yolk
That causes everyone to choke:

The butler and the parlour maid
And footman? For when eggs are laid
You should refrigerate them soon
(And most especially in June,

July and August) or they'll rot
And then you know what you have got?

A stomach ache and temperature
And ailments that you cannot a cure.

The hen whose eggs you have consumed
Will chortle as you lie there doomed
And cluck at you and poke and peck
Till angrily you wring its neck.

But that will not alleviate
The symptoms that you would placate.
Your fit of ire is frowned upon
By every elder alderman,

By all your guests and servants who
Will cluck their tongues like chickens do.
Come, come! The hasty violent act
Is barbarous and cruel, in fact!

So what then? Would you dare attempt
To strangle those who with contempt
Are forced to witness your decline?
You wail and moan and screech and whine

And drink like any alcoholic,
Trying to relieve your colic,
Searing twinge and throbbing pain
And all that drumming in your brain.

No, let me give you sound advice:
Eschew the egg. It will suffice
That you restrict yourself to greens,

Potatoes, carrots, beets and beans

(Though, do be careful of this last.
Your friends may not withstand the blast).
A few extol the man who tries
Abstaining from both flans and pies.

But everyone esteems much finer
Any truly eggless diner.

Nonsense Poetry

There is also a tradition in English and American poetry of nonsense poems. Probably the most famous of these is "Jabberwocky," by Lewis Carroll:

'Twas brillig, and the slithy toves
Did gyre and gimble in the wabe;
All mimsy were the borogoves,
And the mome raths outgrabe.

"Beware the Jabberwock, my son
The jaws that bite, the claws that catch!
Beware the Jubjub bird, and shun
The frumious Bandersnatch!"

He took his vorpal sword in hand;
Long time the manxome foe he sought—
So rested he by the Tumtum tree,
And stood awhile in thought.

And, as in uffish thought he stood,
The Jabberwock, with eyes of flame,
Came whiffling through the tulgey wood,
And burbled as it came!

One, two! One, two! And through and through
The vorpal blade went snicker-snack!
He left it dead, and with its head
He went galumphing back.

"And hast thou slain the Jabberwock?
Come to my arms, my beamish boy!
O frabjous day! Callooh! Callay!"
He chortled in his joy.

'Twas brillig, and the slithy toves
Did gyre and gimble in the wabe;
All mimsy were the borogoves,
And the mome raths outgrabe.

Limericks

Possibly the most popular form of humorous verse is the limerick. The limerick is a five-line poem that has the rhyme scheme a-a, b-b, a. The meter is variable, but generally follows a pattern where the first two lines and the last have eight or nine syllables and the third and fourth lines have five. You can get a sense of the rhythm of it by reading the following examples. Edward Lear wrote scores of the things and here's an example of some of his:

> There was an Old Man with a beard,
> Who said, 'It is just as I feared!
> Two Owls and a Hen,
> Four Larks and a Wren,
> Have all built their nests in my beard!'

> There was an Old Man with a nose,
> Who said, 'If you choose to suppose,
> That my nose is too long,
> You are certainly wrong!'
> That remarkable Man with a nose.

> There was an Old Man on a hill,
> Who seldom, if ever, stood still;
> He ran up and down,
> In his Grandmother's gown,
> Which adorned that Old Man on a hill.

And here are a couple of other examples:

Jemima and Ferdinand Ippi
Were married (though he was a hippy).
She left him one day
In the U.S. of A.
For she loathed to be called Mississippi.

A professor who hailed from Duquesne
Had a very impractical bresne.
His sister's a builder

He very near killed her
By flipping a switch on her cresne.

Chapter 9 – Sharing Poetry

As we mentioned before, the essence of poetry is communication. It's true that you should practice writing poetry and read other people's poetry in order to improve. But there will come a time when you have mastered a degree of skill and are ready to show your work to the world.

Sounding Boards

It is useful if you can find someone to mentor you, or failing that at least someone who will give you an opinion on what there is about your poetry that works, or doesn't work. What is most valuable is if you can find someone who will give you advice about how a poem can be improved. This is preferably someone who has some experience in the area, maybe another more experienced poet, or a teacher of English. But if you can't find an expert, at least find someone who is prepared to be honest.

At first, taking criticism can be hard. But one way to mitigate the risk of your punching them in the jaw is if you initially view all the poems you write as "practice" rather than the finished article. It takes practice to perfect the art of writing poetry so there is no shame in admitting to yourself and to your reviewer that you are only learning. This helps you not to place too much of your self-worth in your poems and hopefully leaves you more open to receive constructive suggestions.

Also, just because you have asked somebody for an opinion on your poetry, does not mean that you have to accept everything they say as true. No need to lie down on the floor like a doormat and invite them to walk all over you! You can simply thank them for their comments and then make your own decision as to whether you think they are right or not.

Poetry Groups

When I was learning how to write poetry I was fortunate enough to have a few friends who also had an interest in poetry. We used to meet every few weeks to discuss our work. We would each distribute copies of a poem we had written. We would then read out the poem and have the others in the group give comments. It is rather daunting to sit there tight-lipped while, potentially, a room full of people criticizes the work you spent ages trying to perfect. So we had a set of rules that alleviated the burden.

- After the person had read out the poem, he or she got a chance to say what they thought was good about it – what worked well.
- Next, the others in the group would give positive feedback, saying what they liked about the poem.
- After that, the author would get to criticize his or her own poem, stating what didn't work so well or could be improved.
- Lastly, the group got to make comments on any improvements that they saw as necessary.

These rules had the dual advantage that everyone

was pretty much forced to say something positive about the poem, and also it allowed the author to preempt criticism by stating up-front what could be improved.

Online Forums

If you can't find anyone else to help you with your poetry, you can always join an online forum. This is like a virtual group where the members submit poems and receive comments from other members. It is not hard to track down these forums. The only thing to watch out for is that some of the forums and sites only seem to give positive feedback and are a bit of a mutual admiration society. Nothing wrong with that necessarily, since everyone needs some encouragement. And there is a faint thrill you get when you see your poem published on the Internet. But if you are serious about producing good poetry and value honest feedback, there are a number of websites that are aimed at peer review and mutual support, so the chance of getting honest constructive criticism is higher.

Poetry Readings

It can be quite entertaining attending poetry readings, where several authors read out their poems. Poems almost always sound better when read aloud. To that extent, it can be a very valuable experience giving a poetry reading yourself or contributing to one. It gives you confidence in your work and, provided you practice before hand, can elicit a very positive response from the audience.

It can be a bit nerve-racking at first, but can be a boost to your morale. If you are serious about writing poetry, it is very useful, if not essential, to find somewhere where you can read your poetry to an audience, even if it's just to your family or a few close and sympathetic friends.

Blogs and Websites

If you are ready to share your poetry with other people in a more public way, why not start a poetry blog. A blog would allow you to post poems as and when you write them and it would also allow you to invite comments from other people. It also has the advantage of being an online repository of your poetry that shows your progress over time.

To the same extent the content doesn't have to be all poems, you could intersperse actual poems with other blog posts in which you share what you've learned about poetry or discuss various poets, or the poetry scene in general. Each time you write a blog post you can advertize the fact on Facebook and Twitter.

Or, you could go the whole hog and start your own website. The only drawback with this is that you would have to pay an annual fee for the domain name and also perhaps fees to the company that hosts you site on their servers.

Poetry Magazines

The traditional way of publishing poetry is to

submit your poems to magazines and journals in the hope of a positive response. Obviously, what you submit has to be pretty good in most cases, although often enough you see poetry published which is not quite as good as you'd expect.

Many periodicals insert poetry in the space left over at the end of an article. It is probably easier and you will have more chance of success if you choose small local magazines to submit to first. It can be a great boost to your confidence to have some published poems under your belt. Pay attention to whether the magazine you submit to prefers formal poetry (rhyming and metered) or free verse. More and more journals and beginning to consider traditional forms again, such as the sonnet. Nowadays, many magazines have websites where you can view archived editions to see what the poetry looks like and whether it is in a style that you are capable of.

Some magazines accept email submissions, others require you to submit your poems via an online submission system. But a lot of magazines still won't accept submissions except through regular mail.

Again, some magazines do not accept simultaneous submissions – that is, if you have already submitted your poems to another periodical and have still not received a response. Others do accept simultaneous submissions provided you tell them as soon as your work has been accepted somewhere else.

If you go onto the website of any of the magazines you are targeting, they almost always have a page that gives their "Submission Guidelines." There you will find out details such as: how many poems to submit and in what format, how long you can expect to wait for a reply; whether you need to include a self-addressed envelope with your submission (which is nearly always the case with snail mail submissions), where to send your poems and to whom and so on. Pay attention to these guidelines, since it could make the difference between being considered for publication or having your submission thrown out, out of hand, because you didn't follow them.

I also find that it's useful to keep a spreadsheet database of what poems I have submitted to what magazines, just so I don't get confused.

Poetry Competitions

One way of sharing your poetry with other people, which can also be financially rewarding if you are lucky or outstandingly brilliant, is by entering poetry competitions and contests. Some poetry competitions have a submission fee of a few dollars. Others are free. But many of these contests are run every year by these organizations so it is worth checking each year, for the current year's entry deadlines.

Publishing Your Poetry

It used to be the case that a poet had to have poems published in a whole variety of magazines before a publisher would even consider publishing a book of his or her poetry. It was also the case that if you couldn't find a publisher, but still wanted to publish your poems as a book, you had to pay for the whole shebang – the typesetting, the design, the cover art, the printing, the marketing, everything.

Nowadays with Print On Demand services you can print your poems in book form without paying a dime for the set up. Similarly, you can also sell your work online as an e-book.

(NB. For more information on how to independently publish your poetry you might like to try "How to Publish Your Book: A Beginner's Guide" in the same series)

Chapter 10 – Conclusion

In this book we have defined what a poem is, how to choose a subject for your poem, and the various techniques you can combine to produce a successful poem. We also looked at what is required to produce a good poem, compared formal verse and free verse, and surveyed a handful of the different types of poem that are available. And lastly, we discussed how you can share your poetry with others, because, after all, poetry is principally about communication.

Many people are vague about poetry and recoil from stating exactly what a poem is and how you can tell if it is any good or not. In this book I have tried to be as specific as possible, without being dogmatic. I hope you have enjoyed read through these chapters.

If you have an interest in other kinds of writing as well, please check out my other volumes in this series, which are listed at the end of this book.

Sean O'Neill

ABOUT THE AUTHOR

Sean O'Neill has a Master of Arts degree in English from Glasgow University. He has had poetry published in a variety of magazines and has published five books of poetry and two books of light verse. As well as being a poet, he is a writer and translator and has published six novels and four non-fiction books.

Poetry books:
this stage of life
Casting a line
The snipe in winter
The Hunting of the bees
Black Dog
Cautionary Verses for Childish Adults
Clever Limericks for Childish Adults

Novels:
Lab Rat
Four Degrees
Muscle for Hire
The Blood Menagerie
Milano
Freighted

Non-fiction
How to Write a Poem: A Beginner's Guide
How to Write a Novel: A Beginner's Guide
How to Write a Non-fiction book: A Beginner's Guide
How to Publish Your Book: A Beginner's Guide

All of his books are available on Amazon and elsewhere.